DO THE RIGHT THING!

HONESTY

Written by Margaret Snyder
Illustrated by Kathy Mitchell

ROURKE BOOK CO., INC.
VERO BEACH, FL 32964

Printed in the United States of America.

Library of Congress Cataloging-in-Publication Data

Snyder, Margaret.
     Honesty / Margaret Snyder.
          p.   cm. — (Doing the right thing)
Summary: Illustrations and simple text provide examples of being honest in everyday life.
     ISBN 1-55916-232-5
     1. Honesty—Juvenile literature. [1. Honesty.]   I. Title.
II. Series.
BJ1533.H7S68   1999
179'.9—dc21   98-48391
                                                                                          CIP
                                                                                          AC

HONESTY

Honesty is telling the truth
even when it is hard to do.

4

Honesty is playing fair in your
favorite card game.

When you give someone back the money
she has dropped, that is honesty.

Honesty is cleaning your room and not hiding your toys under the bed.

Working on your own test paper
shows you are honest.

Honesty is brushing your teeth when you have promised to brush them.

11

An honest person calls her friends to find out who lost the bicycle.

13

When you tell someone about your fears you are being honest.

Honesty is showing your mom and
dad you love them.

16

Emily is being honest when she says trucks
are her favorite toys even though some kids
tease her.

An honest person admits when he
needs help with his computer.

Honesty is telling the neighbors
how their window got broken.

20

When you return the skates
you borrowed from a friend,
that is honesty.

Honesty is giving back the
adorable puppy to the little
girl who lost her pet.

24

Honesty is wearing your hat and mittens because you told your mom you would wear them.

Tom is being honest when he says,
"Excuse me, I already have one,"
when he is handed a second treat.

Honesty is going back to the store to pay
for the candy that you accidentally took
from the counter.

An honest person waits her turn in line
instead of sneaking in front of people
ahead of her.

The story of how George Washington told his father that he had chopped down the cherry tree shows that our first president believed in honesty. He set an example for all of us.

31

You Are Honest!

These steps can help you be more honest. But do NOT write in this book; use a sheet a paper.

1. **How do you show honesty?** Write 4 ways.
   I don't fib or lie to stay out of trouble.
   I ask if I can use others' things.
   I pay for everything I take from a store.
   I don't act like a hero or a star.

2. **Do you ever act dishonest?** If so, write 2 ways that you show dishonesty.
   I play computer games in my room instead of assigned schoolwork.
   I talk about other kids' bad grades. It makes my grades look better!
Which one seems easier to stop? Draw a star beside it.

3. **Can you stop it?** How can you turn this dishonesty into honesty? Count the ways on your fingers. Stop at 5.

4. **Start today.** Look in the mirror and make a speech:
"I will be more honest. First, I will _____. Then I will _____." Say all the ways you thought of.

5. **Start each day right.** Say, "I am an honest person." Say it often during the day, too.

6. **Write these words every evening:**
   Today I showed honesty when _____.
Fill in the blank. Use the same paper every time. Keep it up for 2 weeks or more.

7. **Do step 2 again sometime.**